MADE-UP MUCK ?

A tall tale or a small tale about life on an Orkney farm

Words and pictures by

Britt Harcus

Printed at The Orcadian Limited, Hell's Half Acre, Hatston, Orkney, Scotland

www.orcadian.co.uk

ISBN 1-902 957-25 -3

Acknowledgements

Firstly I would like to thank James Miller and the staff at

The Orcadian Limited for all their help and patience.

My tutors at the National College of Art and Design

(NCAD), Dublin, also deserve a big thank you for their

advice and inspiration over the past few years.

And my parents deserve a huge medal for their constant

encouragement and support.

Finally, thanks to everyone else who has helped me

produce this book - you know who you are!

For everyone at Quanterness - my home farm in Orkney
- and to all other farmers who battle against the odds.

I hope this brings some sunshine to your day...

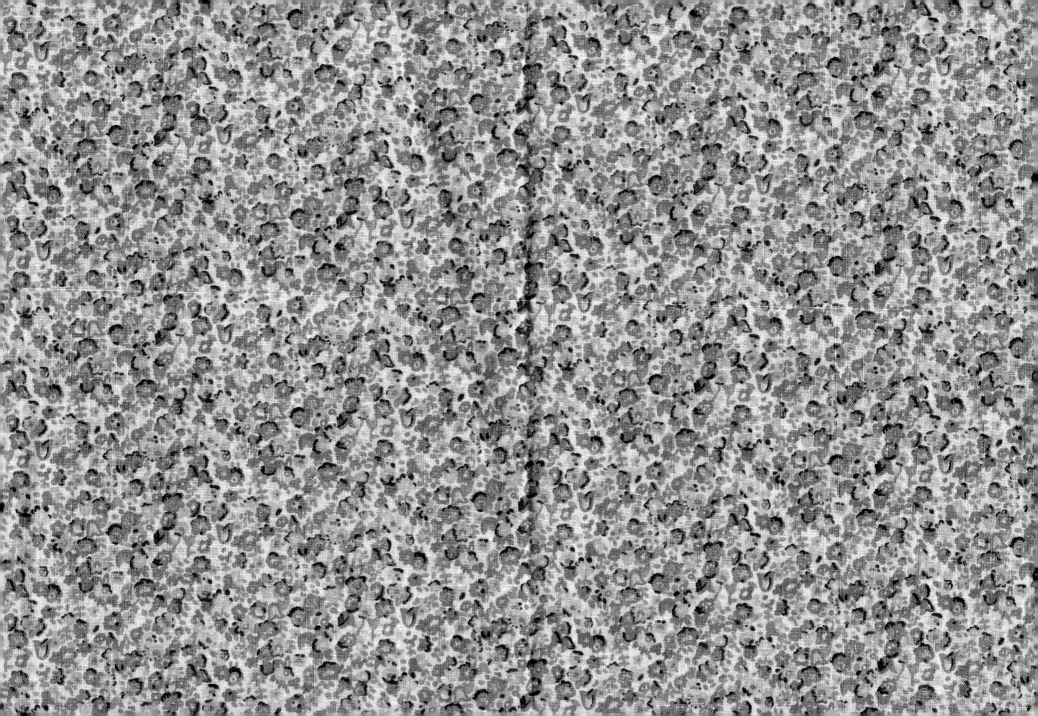

FARMING

Mucky boots, silly animals and maybe even dozy
Old MacDonald...?

WRONG!

Here's the real story about life on the farm...

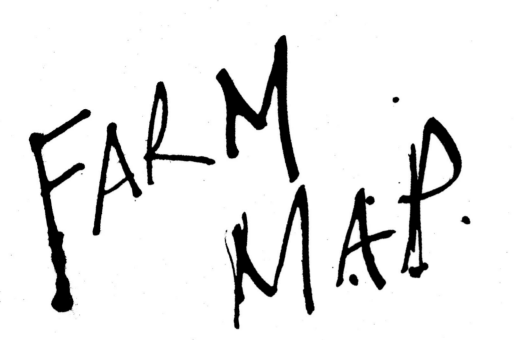

FARM MAP.

This map shows a typical farm layout. Plenty of sheds for storage and shelter, plus fields for the animals and crops...oh, and not forgetting a big, stone built house for the farmer to stay in.
Can you see where the farmer keeps his cows?

FARMERS

(No sign of Old MacDonald here – they can have names like Scott, Richard or even Hilda)

Farmers are BUSY folk who sometimes get a bit stressed with all the work they have to do...

Why?

They rely on the weather for success. When it's raining for weeks they need some sunshine and when it's dry for days they're desperate for a shower. It drives them nutty!

Things you should know about a farmer in case you find one...

- Farmers watch the weather forecast daily

- They need tea and digestive biscuits every day to keep them happy

- They like hot homemade soup

- They never wear gloves

- OR go on a proper holiday

Just like cattle, there are different breeds of farmers (not available to buy in shops)...

Beef farmers

Dairy farmers

Arable farmers

Pig farmers

And mixed farmers who tend both their animals and the land.

Arable farmers grow vegetables and crops...can you guess what the other farmers do?

ANIMALS

Animals can't talk, so they need a lot of care and attention to make sure everything's OK for them. Like a baby – except much bigger!

If you are lucky enough to meet a farm animal remember that they hate...

- Fireworks
- Strange meal times
- Being spoken to in a silly voice or worse still...
- Being SHOUTED at!

COWS

Taking a closer look at the animals...
Firstly let's see the cows. None silly or mad here!

Cows have furrrrrry ears, wet muzzles and gorgeous long eyelashes.

Beef cows come in lots of different colours such as brown, cream or even red (my dad says black ones are the best though).

Dairy cows are normally a sort of black and white patchy colour. They give us milk for cheese, butter and scrummy yogurt.

Clever girls eh?

Next up are those wooooolly creatures...

Sheep can look stunned, shocked and a bit scared at times. They are not. They are fine.

They have thick woolly coats, which are sheared off in the warmer weather – don't worry their coats grow back. The wool is used to make hats, scarves and socks for us.

SHEEP

(SNOOZE)

Males are called rams, females are called ewes and their babies are called lambs.

Farmers can get pretty stressed about their
sheepish ladies because in spring time all the
lambs seem to arrive at the same time and usually
at funny times of the day and night.

No sleep for farmers like Hilda during these few
weeks...

PIGS

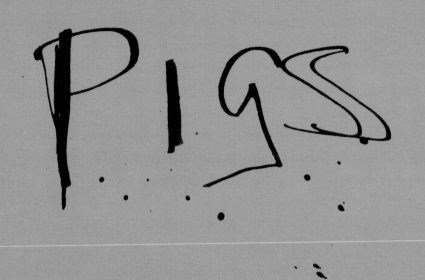

Pigs are smelly animals. They are lazy lumps with big bellies. They'll eat anything!

They have curly tails, little legs and beady eyes.

Famous pigs include movie star *Babe* and of course the *Three Little Pigs* who battled with a wolf over a place to stay.

However, normal pigs you may see in the field
are important too. Females give birth to large
litters of around seven or eight piglets at a time.

HENS

Hens have feathers not fur. They also have sharp peck-peck beaks and claws. They enjoy eating grains and seeds and scratching in gravel. Baby hens or *chicks* are beautifully coloured bright yellow. They come from the eggs laid by the mother hen. Hens also give us eggs so we can enjoy yummy boiled eggs for breakfast. *Free range eggs are best.* It means the hen had a nice place to stay while making the egg.

CHICK-

Chicker

CHICKI-

Sheepdogs are trained to round up the sheep. It
saves the farmer running all over the countryside.

BUT sometimes the dogs decide to take matters
into their own paws and chase our woolly friends.

ANY OTHER ANIMALS?

Handsome horses,

tiny mice,

several cats,

a dozy donkey

smelly rats,

a few old geese,

a couple of turkeys,

a duck,

a drake,

some fleas

some flies,

rabbits

chicks,

ticks and

goats...

This list ranges from farm to farm but
covers most types of beasts, large and small.

But you must always remember that every bird
and animal on the farm has a purpose. Some
even end up on the dinner table...

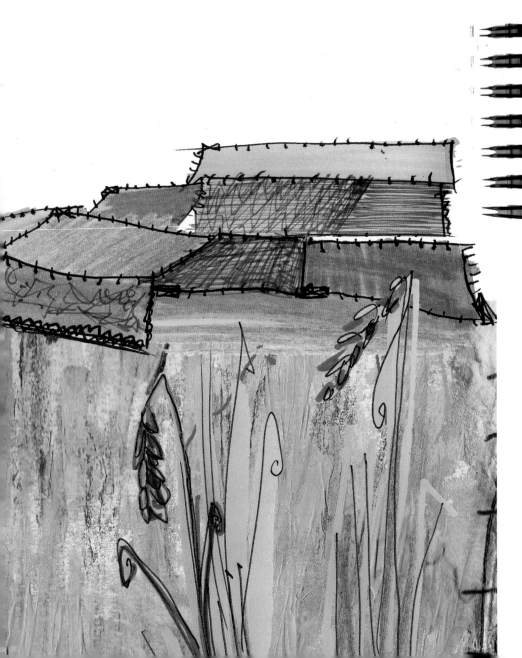

Arable farmers grow crops and look after the land. Barley, oats, wheat, oilseed rape and corn fill their fields. Try to find out a bit more about these crops...to start you off, did you know that oilseed rape is really mega bright yellow when it's in flower?

You might need your sunglasses to see it!!!

Potatoes,

   sweet potatoes,

      swedes,

turnips,

   carrots,

      beetroot,

         parsnips,

brocolli,

   cabbage,

and

last but not least flowery

   cccccc cauliflower.

These are just some of the
scrummy vegetables that grow
from the land.

Draw a parsnip in the space above...

MACHINERY

All farms have different types of machinery to make the workload easier for the farmers. This can include vehicles like diggers, quadbikes and landrovers. Keep your eyes peeled for a yellow digger or a blue landrover next time you are in the countryside.

Tractors play a huge part in farming. They come
in loads of colours (my big brother says red
tractors are the best) and they can be used for
ploughing, pulling, transporting and towing – plus
they have CD players so you can listen to tunes in
the tractor now too!

Most farms have a workshop for repairs and a
scrap metal heap for junk too.

Different times of the year need different machinery...

- ploughs and rollers in spring

- mowers and trailers in summer

- autumn time needs a combine harvester

- and a tractor and trailer is needed by winter time to feed the cows

MADE-UP MUCK?

No chance...This storybook is no fairytale. It's a tiny look at real life on a funky farm with no trace of Old MacDonald. Find out more about farming before the next book in the series...

And remember...

- Always close the gate – it stops the cows from escaping

- Wear your wellies with pride

- Watch out for the earrings on the next cow or sheep you see – these tags are used to tell the farmer which animal is which

- Ask the next horse you meet to see it's passport! They each have a book all to themselves so if they travel they get it stamped just like we do – cool eh?

- And finally fish! Yes, fish live on a farm but it's a completley different kind all together...

The End!

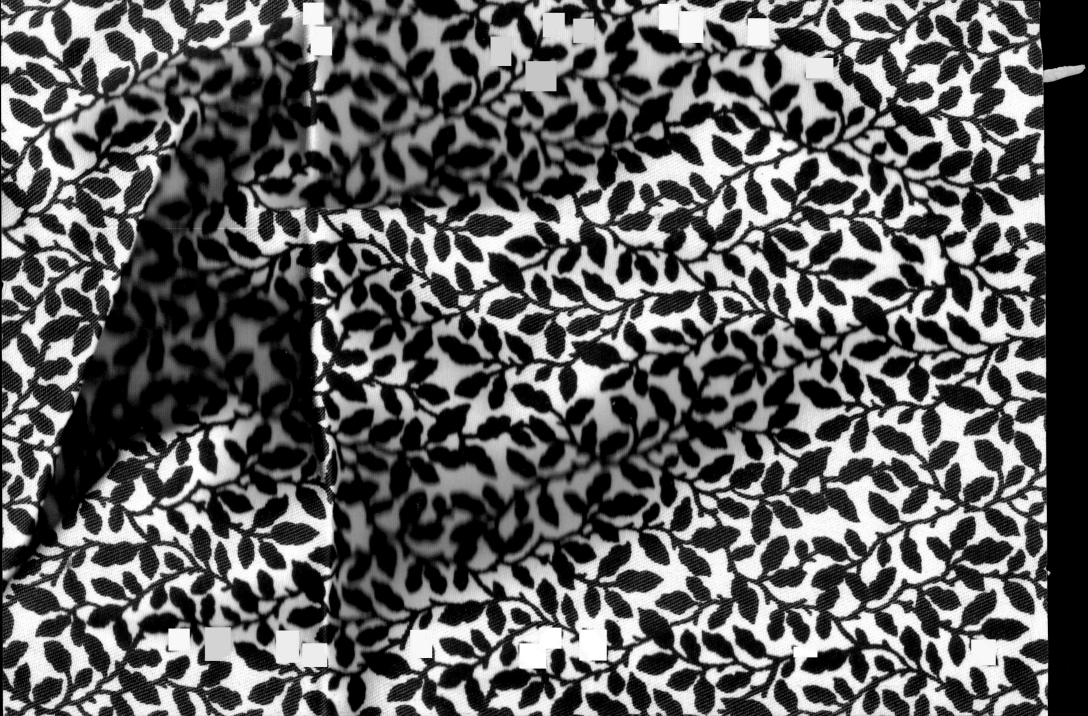